Start a Short-Haul Trucking Business

Be Your Own Boss and Work from Home

Trucking Business Startup: Get a CDL and Change Your Life!

Joe Billingsley

Published by:

Valley Of Joy Publishing Press

COVER & INTERIOR DESIGN

BY

RACHEL FRIEDMAN

FIRST EDITION

Contents

Introduction

Everyone is aware of the trucking industry and the purpose it serves. We all drive past those big rigs on the freeway, taking goods from point A to point B. Perhaps you've even given thought to the idea of driving a truck; the freedom of the open road and being your own boss sounds intriguing.

But what if you don't like the idea of being away from home for long periods of time or think that getting into the business of long-haul trucking is too challenging? You may not be aware that a great alternative and growing trend is short-haul trucking. That's what I'm going to discuss with you in this book.

First, we're going to look at what short-haul trucking is and how it's different from long-haul trucking. Then we'll help you to see if short-haul trucking is right for you. Then we'll look into how you can get started with short-haul trucking and grow it into a successful business. So let's get started.

Own Your Business. Why Do You Need That?

At the very beginning of this book, I really want us to agree on one thing. This is very simple, but I'd like you to have a mindset that goes thus: "For whoever seeks will always find. I sincerely wish to find information and will try my utmost best to put it to good use." I'd like you not only to read all the pages but flip through with the thought: "This won't be later, now is the right time."

Well, are you ready? Let's start!

Now it is not difficult to start your own business. It has never been and never will be difficult. In general, doing what you want is easy. But it is often hard to know what you really want. To solve this puzzle, you need to ask yourself: "Why do you need your own business?" This is the very first question that needs to be answered with the utmost honesty.

For example, a person may open a beauty salon just to be able to have small talk at work because this is what they like. In this scenario, there will be a business and also an element of pleasure. Just like with this example, a business, especially a small one related to the service sector, is the same. No offices, but a constant presence on the spot, working with clients and supporting the team. Communication, motivation, prioritization, goal setting and systematization of processes, automation and again communication.

So, I repeat the question: why do you need your own business? I am not the final authority, and you may not agree with me. But I would like to hear at least one of these answers from you: self-realization, freedom of action, and a brilliant business idea, I have vast experience and skills, and I am ready to start working for myself; I want to employ others, I am ripe for decision-making, and for full control of my own life, I am ready to take responsibility for people. Something like this. On condition that at least 2 answers from this list are yours, you can proceed to action. This should be your motivating force that should keep you going over the years.

And then, where does every business start? With an idea and a business plan. But before writing a business plan, I have a suggestion for you. Answer honestly the questions that I will now ask you. Based on the answers, we will understand: write a business plan or, well, simply follow the tips in this book and go straight to business.

Question #1: What business idea am I running with?

Once upon a time, someone invented a bicycle. Once upon a time, someone invented matches. Someone came up with the idea of brewing coffee beans at the end of the 14th century, coffee began to be delivered worldwide, and now it ranks top ten in sales on the world market. This point here is that everything on the planet was once the first time and began with a thought, with an idea.

But in 2023, finding something new is no longer enough. First, it is very difficult to reinvent the wheel. Second, even if you do discover something new, it may be very difficult to make the idea a success. This is because, in our time, the market is so large, and competition is growing at such an incredible rate that most customers simply stick with the big names they already know and trust. There are too many options, so they simply go for the top ones.

Take an example of you wanting to start your own short-haul trucking business. Not only will you have to invest a colossal amount of money, but you will try to win other companies' clients by all means: increasing the work schedule, price flexibility, increasing customer loyalty with the help of special discounts and gifts, creative PR campaigns, magic... Haha. I could endlessly list what you have to do just to survive this. That's why I added a twist at the end. Essentially, short-haul trucking is a very narrow niche business. It is famous, and it is important, but, in this case, it is best to work with an established firm and have a franchise of sorts.

So, don't think too much; you don't have to worry about what you can change in this business niche. You needn't worry about what ways you can be unique.

Question #2: Will I physically be able to?

Five days a week, you go to work from 9:00 to 5:00. Then you come home and are very tired. Work takes all the power. Leaving the office doors, you turn off your brain - you are tired. Saturday and Sunday are consistently weekend days, and you turn off your cell phone to relax.

Now imagine that you have a two or three-year race ahead of you for a more difficult distance. First year: seven days a week from 8:30 a.m. to 6:00 p.m. Get inventory, work on the inventory, create, worry, realize mistakes, remake, don't give up, don't give up, pay salaries, save on everything for the sake of paying off rent and utility bills, running to deliver on time, staff meeting, smiling with clients, resolving conflicts and smiling again.

In the second year and third years, you will move to five days a week and, most likely, the schedule will be easier - from 10:00 to 8:00, but the worries and physical activities will remain the same; you will just have learned to use your time better and more efficiently; otherwise you will fizzle out.

Are you ready for this? You can't turn off your brain by walking out the door of the office, just as you can't forget about your child. In the subcortex, you think about your business constantly, even when it seems that you are not thinking. You will not be able to disconnect from the process on Saturday and Sunday, and on vacation in other countries, you will constantly catch new ideas, pick up trends and trends and think-think-think how to increase your fleet size, improve, expand, and develop.

And if you have already harnessed yourself to your trucking business, then do not expect that in six months, it will suddenly become passive, and you will calmly wake up at 12:00 and work once a week for the proceeds. Perhaps you will establish and automate all processes very quickly, but not faster than one and a half to two years; these are observations from the experience of my and my friends.

So, prepare yourself. Prepare your husband or wife and children, grandmothers and relatives. Explain that you need a year or two to put everything on track. If you have young kids like me, find a good preschool or nanny. Prepare in advance and keep in mind the idea that such a schedule will not last long and soon everything will return to normal; only at the same time will you still have a successful and efficient business that brings income to your family and enjoyment to you, and you will be one business wiser.

Question #3: Am I passionate about my idea?

Some time ago, a close friend of mine asked me a question: "What do you get high from?". It seems to be a simple question, but it turned out to be difficult to answer it. Catherine ... I confess; honestly, I do not use. And I don't. For most people, the word "high" is equal to the word "pleasure." And if you look in the dictionary, then this word is inevitably associated with drugs or sex. I certainly get pleasure from communicating with my beloved man, but this is definitely not what my friend was talking about. The happiness of communicating with children is also undeniable, but this is also not what she was referring to. She just noticed that I was almost always exceptionally happy, and this seemed off to her.

So, are you passionate about your business idea? Do you love the service that you are willing to begin? Do people need it? Will it make them even a little happier? After all, if you are going to do a job that is very important if you yourself do not believe in it, it will be difficult for you. Not only difficult but very difficult. So, find something to ignite the flame in you. Get "high." Do it when you're on fire. Your flame will serve as a remarkable motivation, make you wake up with the sunrise, move mountains and turn the world upside down.

And this is our human miracle - to burn with an idea. We are endowed with this superpower, which animals rarely have. This fire will keep you happy and will help you keep expanding and scaling.

Question #4: Am I ready to infringe on myself for the sake of business in the next two years?

It is said that a business is opened in order to earn money and improve life. But there are some harsh truths about business. If you want to create a stable long-term business and not a one-day office, you will have to invest, expand, and improve. The word "reinvestment" will have to enter your everyday life. Let me explain a little.

Initially, there are always investments in the project, then you start delivery, maybe by yourself. And then you start to get profits. And then the question arises - what to spend on? Well, if you invest the profit again in your business for expansion or improvement, this is reinvestment. The diagram looks like this:

Investment → project creation → profit → reinvestment.

How long to reinvest in a project depends only on the goals and timing. What do you ultimately want to achieve? In my case, this has been happening for 5 years now. I keep reinvesting. And it's not just fleeting purchases. My goal is absolutely conscious and written down. I copy it from year to year in every next diary. The goal is very simple: expand the fleet, have a stable passive income, and maybe then will I think about a house by the sea, a beautiful, huge and bright apartment. Of course, in my diary - this is a whole essay. For you, a little shortened and in one sentence.

I have no spontaneous desire to change my personal car. I know that a van or a truck can fetch me more money, so I'd buy that instead... And most importantly - I will not take a loan for it; I will go and buy it with saved-up money. This does not mean that I do not spend at all. I spend. Just systematic. At the moment, I drive a simple car, and it does not infringe on my ego. I know I can afford a luxury car, but I won't. I am quite satisfied with my nimble and small economy-class machine.

I want you to remember my words about reinvestment. And when money from your own business begins to flow into your hands, you will sit down for a cup of tea and weigh the pros and cons of your personal spending. Think about what your business will need to get bigger and better. Give it at least two years, wisely pour funds into expansion, and it will answer you with double financial gratitude.

Question #5: Am I ready to take responsibility for myself and for other people?

Some young entrepreneurs think that owning a business means power and money. But while there is money to be made, quite frankly, power over people is somewhere outside of a small business that runs trucks.

In this type of small business, you have a huge responsibility for your team and for the people who came to work for you.

You will be their mom and dad at the same time, plus a personal psychologist and a teacher, and at the same time, keep the limits and not let them get too close to you and into your life, demand the fulfillment of duties, and balance on edge. And also learn to part ways. This is also part of your "responsibility." For example, I do not forgive only one thing - theft. Not a single chance.

Naturally, during the course of business, you will face difficulties, such as days when you have fewer loads to deliver or having to work on Thanksgiving and other holidays. But these small obstacles are nonsense compared to large-scale ones: the financial crisis, the growth of competitors and ugly competition.

These types of large scales crises are very unlikely to affect you. In fact, during the height of the COVID pandemic, my team and I had much more work to do. This directly translated to more income for us all. This was in stark contrast to what most other people were facing at the time.

Being responsible for a team means being able to be ready for periods of ups and downs and be able to hold your team together irrespective of where you currently are.

What is Short-haul Trucking?

Trucking is both a rewarding and stable career choice with plenty of job security. However, most people don't want to go into trucking because of the isolation and long time on the road. This is why short-haul trucking offers the perfect combination of freedom on the road and the stability of extra time at home.

Short-haul trucking is often limited to transporting shipments within a 150-mile radius. This means that short-haul truckers are able to stay closer to home. This also means that routes are brief, so truckers can often complete multiple routes within a day. This breaks up the monotony of driving for long hours and prevents long periods of sitting, which can be bad for your health. Even though short-haul truckers may have long hours, they often have a better work-life balance than other truck drivers. If you think short-haul trucking is for you, then there are two types of short-haul trucking to consider.

Types of Short-haul Trucking

Short-haul trucking is often further divided into two main categories: regional and local. Local truckers often take smaller shipments that take less than 100 miles to deliver, while regional truckers can travel 100 to 250 miles. While this distance may not seem like a big difference, there is a lot to consider when choosing which version of short-haul trucking is right for you.

Regional Trucking

Regional trucking can be similar to long-haul trucking in the fact that drivers may sometimes cross state lines and drive for days. In fact, some regional truckers drive trucks with cabins so they can sleep during long trips. Other drivers choose to stay at hotels. However, regional trucking is different from long-haul trucking because it has more predictable schedules. These regular routes allow drivers to develop better client relationships with the same customers.

Local Trucking

Local truckers often stay within a specific neighborhood, such as transporting from distribution centers to local destinations. Other drivers focus on transporting regional specialties. These drivers often stay on city roads, which is less stressful than driving on highways. They also often drive smaller trucks to make urban navigation easier.

How Short-haul Trucking is Different

While both short and long-haul trucking are similar, there are some key differences to consider when choosing which is best for your career goals. Let's look at these key differences to help you make a decision.

Time on the Road

Perhaps the biggest key difference between short and long-haul trucking is the amount of time each driver spends on the road and away from home. When it comes to short-haul trucking, a driver may only work day shifts and be home at the end of each day. When it comes to long-haul trucking, a driver may be away from home and on the road for several days, weeks or even months at a time, depending on the load and the destination. When making your decision, you should consider how much time you're willing to be away from home and family before committing to a trucking position. If you like to travel or prefer to be on the road for an extended period of time, then long-haul trucking may be right for you. However, if you want to stay within your local area or have a family, then short-haul trucking may be the better option for you.

Salary

Another key difference between short and long-haul trucking is the salary they make. When you travel longer distances and spend more time away from home, you can earn a higher salary. The average long-haul trucker makes about $80,000 per year. On the other hand, a short-haul trucker can make about $65,000 a year. Depending on the company you drive for, you may be paid per mile driven, or you may get a base salary per year. However, if you choose to go into business on your own, then you can choose what to charge based on the load and distance you have to travel.

Job Duties

Trucking is about more than simply driving a truck from point A to point B. Both short and long-haul trucking share many of the same job duties, including obeying traffic laws, monitoring loads for security and safety, handling vehicles appropriately and data entry. However, there are still some differences between short and long-haul trucking job duties.

Service Logging

Most truck drivers log their hours of service in order to get paid, but most short-haul truck drivers don't do this. This is because long-haul drivers often spend more time in the truck and driving on the road.

Number of Stops

Short-haul truck drivers can make two to six stops a day, depending on their loads and routes. Long-haul truck drivers may only make one to two stops in a few days to weeks.

Traffic Laws

Long-haul truck drivers spend most of their time on highways, while short-haul truck drivers spend most of their time on city streets. While both need to obey traffic laws, long-haul drivers need to focus more on highway-specific laws that may not apply to short-haul truck drivers.

Vehicle Maintenance

Both short and long-haul truck drivers need to monitor their vehicle maintenance, but the requirements vary for heavier vehicles compared to the smaller and lighter trucks used for short-haul trucking.

Loading and Unloading

Both long and short-haul truckers will assist in loading and unloading the trucks. However, the difference is in how often this happens. Short-haul truckers may need to do this several times per day, while long-haul drivers may only need to do this once a week or so.

Job Training

There are different training requirements for short and long-haul truckers. Both need a CDL or commercial driver's license, but long-haul truckers often need more training to complete longer drives. For long-haul drivers, there is often a three to six-month driving course with the companies they join or through a private truck driving academy. These courses often cover traffic laws, truck operations and specific laws regarding heavy loads and larger vehicles.

Work Environment

Both long and short-haul drivers spend a good amount of their time in temperature-controlled vehicles. However, short-haul drivers may have more exposure to the elements because they make frequent deliveries throughout the day. On the other hand, long-haul drivers are more prone to sleep deprivation because of driving for long periods of time.

Choosing the Right Career

Long and short-haul trucking offer their own career advantages. Depending on your goals, one might be more suitable than the other. When choosing the right career path for you, you'll want to consider the following:

• How much time are you willing to spend away from home? If you are willing to travel for weeks to months, then long-haul might be the choice for you. But if you have a family at home, then you may want to consider short-haul trucking.

• What are your salary goals? Long-haul drivers will often have a higher salary because of the time commitment. Determining what your ideal salary range is can help you determine which type of trucking is right for you.

• What expenses can you afford? Long-haul trucking often requires greater expenses for things like eating, personal care and accommodations if you aren't going to sleep in your truck. Short-haul trucking doesn't have these expenses since you are often home at the end of the day.

The last thing to consider before you focus on the benefits of short-haul trucking is to consider what is making short-haul trucking in demand right now.

Why Short-haul Trucking is in Demand

Now is the best time to consider a career as a commercial truck driver. According to the American Trucking Association or ATA, there is a massive shortage of truck drivers. Simply put, there aren't enough drivers to complete orders and the shortage of short-haul truckers is expected to increase in the coming years.

Within the trucking industry, the average age for a driver is 46, and the median age for other workers is 41. This means that experienced drivers will retire, and additional vacancies will open. To keep pace with the demand created by industry growth and driver retirement, the industry would need to hire about 900,000 new drivers in a decade. This shortage, along with the many benefits of a short-haul trucking career, make it a great option, so let's consider some of the reasons why you should consider becoming a short-haul truck driver.

Is Short-haul Trucking for You?

When it comes to deciding if short-haul trucking is right for you, it is best to consider the pros and cons of short-haul trucking. Let's first consider the pros of this career choice.

Short-haul trucking is considered a flexible career with lots of benefits. Let's look at what benefits you can enjoy if you choose a career as a short-haul trucker.

Familiar Roads

While short-haul truckers don't spend as much time on the road as long-haul truckers, they become experts on the local roads. When a driver is familiar with the terrain, they learn which routes are the fastest, what intersections are easier to navigate in a truck and where there may be potential speed traps. All of this can make for faster delivery and better customer service.

ELD Exemptions

Commercial truck drivers need to log their hours of service or HOS using an electronic logging device or ELD. HOS regulations are responsible for governing the number of hours a trucker needs to rest between driving legs in order to prevent them from falling asleep at the wheel. For long-haul truckers, these restrictions can be difficult if they need to finish a shipment. However, short-haul truckers who travel within a 100 to 150-mile radius don't need to follow HOS requirements. This means they don't need an ELD or keep track of their HOS compliance. While there may be some restrictions based on the vehicle, this exemption can save short-haul drivers both time and money. This exemption holds as long as drivers are able to rest a specific number of hours a week. This means as a short-haul trucker, you have more flexibility when making your driving choices.

Work-Life Balance

The work-life balance for a short-haul trucker is by far better than that of a long-haul trucker. Short-haul truckers can treat trucking like a job, while long-haul truckers often treat trucking as a lifestyle. This means short-haul truckers can also have interests and relationships outside of work. While short-haul truckers may be paid less than long-haul truckers, more home time can often make up for this difference.

Local Drivers

Short-haul trucking means you can stay local and make deliveries in your community. This makes you more familiar with the area and your customers. When you ensure the products arrive on time without any issues, then this increases customer satisfaction. In addition, by being a local driver, you may be able to get discounts on fuel and other costs.

Set Schedules

When you start a career in short-haul trucking, you'll be able to set up a regular schedule for your deliveries. This can help if you are going to be delivering products on a regular basis. It is also helpful when you have items that need to be delivered at specific times. In the end, it helps build good customer relationships.

Cost Effective

Short-haul trucking is a cost-effective option for both the trucker and the person ordering their services. This is often due to the fact that there is less fuel involved. It is also cheaper to get insurance for a short-haul truck since the risk of accidents is often lower. Lastly, short-haul trucking is often cheaper because it doesn't require as much equipment or as expensive of a rig as long-haul trucking.

Develop Relationships

Perhaps the biggest benefit of short-haul trucking is the fact that you are able to build a relationship with local businesses. You'll get to know the businesses and their products well, which can often lead to repeat business.

Local businesses are also more likely to be understanding should a problem occur with delivery since they know you.

However, this doesn't mean there aren't challenges associated with short-haul trucking. Let's take a moment to consider these.

Challenges of Short-haul Trucking

As with any job, short-haul trucking has its own challenges. Let's look at some of the most common challenges associated with short-haul trucking.

Juggling Multiple Routes

Short-haul truckers, whether owner-operated or driving as a part of a regional fleet, are often paid by the mile. If you are stuck in traffic or delayed by construction, then you're losing time that you could have added to another route. When this is compounded over several deliveries, then you can end up losing a lot of money. Planning a more efficient route means being able to complete more trips and get higher mileage pay.

Client Expectations

Customers can sometimes underestimate the issues a short-haul trucker may face getting deliveries completed on time. Clients see a shorter route distance as being more manageable and, as such, expect shipments to not take as long as non-commercial driving times. This can be inaccurate based on route-specific limitations such as bridge clearances. Make sure you set realistic expectations to establish good working relationships and update your clients on their deliveries.

Loading Dock and Asset Tracking Delays

Loading docks and asset tracking is one of the most chaotic parts of short-haul trucking. Distribution centers can be huge, and it can be easy to get lost navigating the lots to look for a trailer or finding a location to unload. Delays can be caused by a number of other factors, including traffic congestion, bad weather and mechanical problems. Since many short-haul truckers are paid by the mile, these delays can be costly. Especially since you can't rush and risk damaging goods.

Loneliness

Even short-haul truckers can experience the feeling of isolation while driving on the road. Avoiding these feelings of loneliness are key to having a successful truck driving career. Even with a better work-life balance than long-haul trucking, short-haul trucking still sees high turnover rates.

Complex Routes

Trucking is a vast and constantly changing industry, which can be difficult for individuals starting out to keep up with the latest information on ideal routes. When you aren't using the most ideal routes, then you won't be using your time and resources as efficiently, and you can even potentially miss delivery deadlines. In addition, if you aren't familiar with route complexities, you can make costly mistakes like getting lost or taking wrong turns.

Competition

The trucking industry is an increasingly competitive industry, which can make it difficult for new companies to stay in business. A lot of trucking companies are cutting costs by hiring inexperienced drivers or using older trucks that are less reliable. This can decrease the quality of service and increase the risk of accidents. Increased competition can also lead to things like lower prices, which can make it difficult for newer short-haul trucking businesses to make a profit.

Long Days

Even short-haul trucking has days that are long and demanding. As a driver you'll have to deal with traffic, bad weather and long hours. This can be difficult on both you and your truck, which can lead to a number of issues, including accidents, and breakdowns, among others. It can also be more difficult to get rest as a short-haul trucker, which can lead to fatigue and mistakes.

Knowing these pros and cons gives you a greater picture of short-haul trucking. Keeping these pros and cons in mind, it can be a good idea to consider whether you should become a short-haul trucker before you choose to start a short-haul trucking business.

Starting a Short-haul Trucking Company

Whether you are experienced or just getting started, you can enjoy extra freedom by becoming an owner-operator and starting your own short-haul trucking business. Owner-operators are those who own their vehicle or vehicles and contract their own shipments. Rather than dealing with fleet dispatches, owner-operators are able to choose shipments that they find more valuable. It also means you can earn full payment for a shipment and make more money per load. However, there is a lot of cost and liability that goes into becoming an owner-operator. Often owner-operators can spend up to 70% of their pay on expenses.

The Whys of Good Business

If you are thinking of starting a short-haul trucking business, then consider the top four reasons why this can be a good business opportunity.

First, there is a major shortage of truck drivers. The forecast is that the trucking industry is going to need about 100,000 drivers in the near future. When you start a short-haul trucking business, you'll be taking advantage of this gap and have plenty of job opportunities.

The trucking industry is also a place that is still open to innovation. If you can establish efficiency in your fleet and use less fuel-intensive routes and logistics, then you'll improve your value to customers. This will increase your advantage over the competition and help your business achieve long-term success.

The trucking industry is considered a backbone of the economy, which makes jobs in the trucking industry nearly recession-proof. As a short-haul trucking business, you'll be transporting goods to stores from warehouses, and this is something that will always be needed.

Lastly, it is easy to start small with a short-haul trucking company and scale up as needed. This means you won't have to invest a lot in order to start turning a profit, and you'll be able to expand your business as demand and profit margins allow.

Starting a trucking company isn't that complicated. It's not that different from starting any other type of small business. You may face higher equipment costs because of the vehicles, and you may need to search a little harder for talented drivers, but the basic principles of starting a short-haul trucking business are the same. So if you've decided that starting a short-haul trucking business is right for you, then let's continue on in this book to see how you can start a short-haul trucking business.

How to Become a Short-haul Trucker

Whether you have driving experience or not, whether you already work as a short-haul trucker and want to expand as an owner-operator, the process is the same. There are several factors to consider and steps to take, but it won't take long to start your career in a short-haul trucking business. In this book, we are going to break down all the steps you need to go from starting out in short-haul trucking on your own to starting a fleet and growing your business into a long-term success. When it comes to getting started, there are going to be nine main areas to consider. We'll look at each of them in detail so you are prepared for each step of the process.

If you haven't already started, then the first thing you need to do is gain driving experience and get your CDL licensing. Nothing can prepare you better for starting a short-haul trucking business than having hands-on driving experience. This may seem obvious, but there is a lot to consider for this step in the process.

The first thing you need to do is obtain a CDL or commercial driver's license. You can do this by attending a private truck driving school or through a trucking company that has its own training program or will sponsor you to attend a CDL school. Obtaining a CDL can cost between $0 and $5,000, depending on the route you go.

A Class A CDL license is required for combination

tractor-trailers, which is the primary type of equipment used in the trucking industry today. There are a few things to keep in mind:

• Some companies will have you sign an employment contract for one to two years in order to get free CDL training and testing.

• You can also do it yourself by attending a truck driving school.

• There are several different classes of CDL, so you'll want to make sure you have the appropriate license for the equipment you plan to operate and the types of loads you intend to transport.

• For more information, you can contact the Federal Motor Carrier Safety Administration or FMCSA and the local state licensing office. They will provide you with training manuals and additional information at no cost.

Some special CDL endorsements that you need to consider are the following:

• If you are transporting two or three trailers in tandem, then you'll need a double and triple endorsement.

• If you plan to transport bulk liquids and gasses in containers of 119 gallons or larger, then you'll need a tanker endorsement.

• If you plan to transport materials classified as hazardous by the US Department of Transportation, then you'll need a hazmat endorsement.

• If you plan to operate a passenger transport vehicle like a bus, then you'll need a passenger endorsement.

If you are completely new to the trucking industry, then you may be advised to gain experience as a company driver first before you start your own trucking company. This is an excellent piece of advice for one main reason. When you first learn to operate a commercial vehicle, it has a steep learning curve and rookie mistakes are bound to happen, such as getting stuck, backing into things and other similar mishaps. You don't want to struggle with these issues while also facing the challenges of operating a trucking business. Consider some of the advantages you can get from driving for a larger company before starting your own business.

• Large carriers provide inexperienced drivers with the training and guidance needed to become successful.

- Large carriers can more easily absorb the cost of mistakes that could easily put a new trucking company out of business.

- You will be able to put all of your focus into learning how to safely operate a truck and stay in compliance with federal regulations without having to divide your attention to running a business.

- You will get experience running tight schedules without violating regulations and/or hours of service.

- You get experience with the costs of operating a commercial vehicle, such as maintenance and fuel.

- You can take more time to learn how a trucking business works through research, trade journals and social media without having to divide your attention.

- You'll be able to spend time developing a network with other drivers and shippers that will be beneficial when you start your own trucking company.

- You'll have time to learn the nation's freight lanes so you'll make better choices about the type of cargo your new company will transport.

• Working with a larger carrier first will help you ensure that trucking is the right business and career for you before you invest large amounts of money and time into starting your own short-haul trucking business.

While you may think two to three years driving for another carrier prevents you from getting into the market and starting your own business, consider it a future business investment. With the benefits above, it is easy to see how your future business can benefit when you gain adequate experience first. After you've gained the necessary experience, then you'll be in a better position to start out your trucking company on the right foot and become successful. Before we start into the second part of starting a short-haul trucking business, let's look a little closer at the truck driving skills you'll want to acquire before starting your business, as well as the skills you'll want to look for when you need to hire additional drivers for your business.

Truck Driving Skills

The right driving skills are essential in the trucking industry for reliable driving and the safety of both yourself and others on the road. You acquire these skills through training and experience on the road. The most practice you have driving will make you better prepared to run your own business and hire the right people. Let's take a moment to consider the valuable skills you need as a truck driver and how you can improve them.

Truck driving skills are essential qualities drivers need

in order to safely operate a large vehicle. These are the skills that will help to keep you motivated while on the road and will help you deliver great results to your customers. Some common skills are things like accurate navigation and long-term focus, but there are also skills that are common throughout other careers, such as organization and communication. Let's look at some of these skills in greater detail.

Safe Driving

The top focus for truck drivers and their companies should be safe driving. Keeping everyone on the road safe is important, especially when you're behind the wheel of a large vehicle. Having plenty of practice behind the wheel will teach you the proper techniques on maneuvering a large truck. Certifications will provide you with the formal knowledge you need to drive a large truck.

Focus

Truck drivers need to stay focused for an extended period of time. This is key not only during nighttime driving but also during peak daytime rush hours as well. Find a strategy for staying focused, such as reducing distractions and/or planning for your trip before you get on the road.

Responsibility

Truck drivers also need to be responsible and, as such, travel accordingly. This means packing necessary supplies such as food and checking the state of the vehicle before heading out on the road. If you are in an unfamiliar area, you should also take the time to acquaint yourself with local maps before getting on the road. Responsibility is a key factor in demonstrating that a driver is ready to complete their tasks.

Organization

Truck drivers need to fill out a lot of necessary documentation, so having good organizational skills is important. This includes logging in for work and providing travel details. Truck drivers are often required to keep detailed records to ensure safe and responsible driving while keeping the driver and company accountable.

Mechanical Knowledge

Most truck drivers will be on the road by themselves. With proper mechanical knowledge, the driver can solve problems without calling for additional assistance. This can help prevent delivery delays and extend travel time.

Cleanliness

A clean truck is a good sign of a responsible and respectful driver. Drivers spend a lot of time in their trucks. It is important to have a clean truck that is organized and free of trash and personal items.

Now that we know some of the key skills a truck driver should have. Let's take a moment to consider how you can improve on these skills.

Improving Driving Skills

There are both formal and informal ways to improve your skills to have more confidence and an easier time while driving on the road. Let's look at some of the ways you can improve your driving skills.

Practice, Practice, Practice

Practicing your driving is the best way to get more comfortable maneuvering a truck. Experiencing the road in other vehicles is also useful so you can learn street signs and determine your best driving style. Adapt how you drive to specific cars and pay attention to the differences so you can have a wider understanding of how you drive.

Learn from Others

Learning from the experience of other drivers can provide you with greater knowledge about truck driving. Experienced drivers might be able to offer tips and rules you don't already know. You can learn these additional tips by talking with other truck drivers.

Stay up to Date on Driving Rules

A useful way to stay knowledgeable is to update yourself on driving laws. Driving rules can change based on location, while other driving rules are highly specific. In addition, laws can change each year, so you want to continually learn about any changes to driving regulations. The more regulations you are familiar with, the better your driving will be.

Additional Skills

In addition to the skills needed when driving a truck, there are also some skills that can help you in the workplace as an employee and employer. They will help you with achieving driving goals and meeting customer demands. Consider these additional skills that can be helpful for truck drivers.

Good Communication

It is vital to have clear and effective communication between drivers and the company they work for. Communication is key to asking questions and having an open dialogue. You may need to explain something to an employee in a way they understand. When there is clear and effective communication, then everyone involved stays informed.

Quick Thinking

The road can be a very unpredictable place, and quick thinking allows you to adjust to unexpected things accordingly. If you need to readjust your route, quick thinking allows you to stay safe and still meet deadlines. Quick thinking needs to be well-informed and involve the entire situation. Productive truck drivers are ones that can exhibit proper judgment in a timely manner.

Alertness

Truck drivers need to stay alert so they can be aware of their surroundings. Alert drivers are distracted and remain goal-oriented with their eyes on the road. If you have to drive at night, you'll need to stay focused. Each driver has their own approach to staying alert, so you should consider what others suggest while also figuring out what works best for you.

Patience

Driving is an experience that requires a lot of patience, especially if you are on the road for a long time. You'll likely experience a lot of traffic changes during a daily route. When you are patient, you'll be able to stay focused on the task at hand and the ability to wait if needed.

Self-Awareness

This means knowing both yourself and how you work. You need to be able to notice when you're tired and when it is necessary to ask for help. If you have self-awareness, then you'll make better decisions because you can consider your current state and needs.

Obtain Licenses and Permits

The right licenses and permits are required for most businesses, but what is required will vary depending on the state, county, and local government requirements. Throughout the United States, there are over 150,000 filing jurisdictions, each with its own requirements. This gives you an idea of how challenging this can be. Depending on the type of trucking company you are starting and where you plan to operate, there can be a number of licenses and permits that apply to you. Some of the common ones that apply to a trucking business include:

A commercial driver's license (CDL)

A USDOT number

An MC number

An International Registration Plan

International Fuel Tax Agreement decal

Let's look at each of these and some others in greater detail to ensure your trucking business is in compliance and legally ready to start work.

CDL

Driving a commercial motor vehicle requires the driver to have greater knowledge, experience, skills, and physical abilities than those who drive non-commercial vehicles. In order to get a CDL or Commercial Driver's License, applicants need to pass both a skill and knowledge test focused on these higher standards. Those who get their CDL are also held to higher standards when operating motor vehicles on public roads. Serious traffic violations can affect the ability of a driver to maintain CDL certification.

Drivers often obtain a CDL from their home state since it is illegal to have a license from more than one state. Special endorsements may also be needed if you or any drivers working for you will be driving the following:

Trucks with double or triple trailers

Trucks with a tank

Trucks carrying hazardous materials loads

Passenger vehicles

Based on Federal standards, states will issue CDLs and Commercial Learner's Permits (CLPs) based on the following classifications:

Class A applies to any combination of vehicles that have a gross combination weight rating or gross combination weight of 26,001 pounds or more, inclusive of a towed unit(s) with a gross vehicle weight rating or gross vehicle weight of more than 10,000 pounds.

Class B applies to any single vehicle with a gross vehicle weight rating or gross vehicle weight of 26,001 pounds or more or any such vehicle towing a vehicle with a gross vehicle weight rating or gross vehicle weight, not over 10,000 pounds.

Class C applies to any single vehicle or combination of vehicles that don't meet the definition of the above classes but is either designed to transport 16 or more passengers, including the driver. It also applies to vehicles designed to transport hazardous materials.

Endorsements and Restrictions

Drivers who operate special classes of commercial vehicles need to pass additional tests to get any of the following endorsements on their CDL:

T - Double/Triple Trailers (Knowledge Test)

P - Passenger (Knowledge and Skills Test)

N - Tank Vehicle (Knowledge Test)

After taking a test, there are also a few restrictions that can be placed on a CDL. It is important to know these when hiring drivers for your company:

L - Drivers who don't pass the Air Brakes Knowledge Test, don't correctly identify the components of the air brake system, don't properly conduct a systems check of the air brake system, or don't take the skills test in a vehicle with an air brake system, will have an L no full air brake restriction on their license.

Z - Drivers who take their test in a vehicle with an air-over hydraulic brake system will have a Z no full air brake restriction on their license. Whether there is an L or Z restriction on the license, the driver is not authorized to operate a commercial vehicle equipped with full air brakes.

E - If the Skills Test is done in a vehicle with an automatic transmission, then an E restriction means no manual transmission is placed on the license.

O - A driver taking a Skills Test in a Class A vehicle with a pintle hook or other non-fifth wheel connection has an O restriction preventing them from driving any Class A vehicle with a fifth-wheel connection.

M - A driver who possesses a Class A CDL but gets their passenger or school bus endorsement in a Class B vehicle gets an M restriction indicating that they can only operate Class B and C passenger vehicles or school buses.

N - A driver who possesses a Class B CDL but gets their passenger or school bus endorsement in a Class C vehicle gets an N restriction indicating that they can only operate Class C passenger vehicles or school buses.

V - If the FMCSA notifies the state that a medical variance is issued to a driver, then the state needs to indicate the existence of the CDLIS driving record and the CDL document with a V restriction code.

Individual states may have additional restrictive categories or have additional endorsement codes not attached to Federal regulations.

Getting a CDL

There are several steps involved in getting a CDL. There are also medical requirements and residency requirements, in addition to knowledge and skills tests.

The first step you need to do is to get a copy of your state's Commercial Driver's Licensing (CDL) Manual. Each state has its own process for getting a CDL, and these manuals will outline the specifics for you.

The second thing you need to do is to determine which type of vehicle you'll be driving and what kind of loads you'll be hauling.

Lastly, you'll need to determine what endorsements or special classifications you need and prepare for any knowledge or skills test related to them.

Once you have done these three things to prepare for your CDL, there are two basic steps to getting your actual license.

The first step you need to do is to get a Commercial Learner's Permit (CLP). This permit only authorizes you to practice on public roads with a qualified CDL holder with you. Getting this permit is more than just passing a knowledge test like a standard driver's license. To ensure you are eligible, your record will be checked for the last 10 years in all 50 states. You will also need to bring proof that you are medically qualified in your state. Most types of commercial driving will require a DOT medical card with a DOT physical. Some states may also require documentation to prove your name and residency. There are also fees associated with a CLP.

The second step is to get your CDL. You'll need to have your CLP for at least fourteen days before you can take the Skills Test for your CDL. Some states will also require CDL training before testing. Before showing up to the test, it is highly recommended that you practice the inspection tests and maneuvers in the CDL manual for your state with a qualified individual. You'll need to pass all three parts of the Skills Test: the Vehicle Inspection, the Basic Controls, and the Road Test.

After passing the Skills Test, you'll need to take the documentation for processing. Some states give you a CDL the same day, while others will send it in the mail. Just make sure everything is correct before you leave since you don't want to fix mistakes later.

Getting your CDL is just the first step in a series of legal paperwork requirements for starting your trucking business. The next focus is on the legal aspects that fall under the trucking authority.

Business Vision and Mission

Before you start working on starting your business, you'll need to have a plan in place and ask yourself a few important questions. The questions will help you come up with a plan for your business and aren't that difficult to answer if you already have a vision for your business.

Where Will You Base Your Business and How Far Will You Haul?

The base location for your business and the states you plan to haul freight in are crucial pieces of information you need to know before starting your business. If you choose to stay within your state, you may not need some licensing and costs associated with hauling freight across state lines. For example, if you plan to haul across state lines, you'll need an MC number, and there are fewer requirements for hauling within your own state.

Will You Do the Driving?

If you want to drive the truck at the start of your business endeavor, then you'll need more licensing. For a one-truck operation, you can save money on employee salary, but you'll still need to make sure you have your commercial driver's license, which does require some work.

Do You Plan to Hire or Contract Drivers?

While you don't have to set up operations in a specific way, you'll need to consider whether you plan to hire employees or work with contractors later on in your business. One of the more difficult tasks of growing your business is to find qualified drivers, and we'll discuss this in greater detail later.

Lastly, you need to ask yourself if you plan on specializing in a niche area. Let's consider why you should choose a niche for your trucking business.

Choose a Niche

The most important step to having a successful trucking business is to choose and support the right niche market. The niche you choose will determine the equipment you purchase, the rate you charge, and the freight lanes you can service. As an owner-operator, you should focus on markets that are avoided by larger carriers. This will give you less competition, and you will still have many markets to focus on; let's consider some of the markets open to you and which one you should choose.

Dry Van

With this option, you have flexible equipment, and you can use it to support several industries. It also presents a low barrier of entry since the equipment isn't very expensive. However, there is a lot of competition in this category. There are a lot of companies with many resources as well as a number of new owner-operators like you who want an easy start in the trucking industry. With all this competition, it is difficult to get a good-paying load and secure regular customers. So if possible, you do well to look into other areas.

Specialized Loads

It is best to choose a niche industry that doesn't have as many competitors. Large carriers tend to avoid specialized loads since they are more complex. This means small fleets and owner-operators can have better success within the specialized load market. The type of specialized loads you focus on will depend on the permits, driving skills, and experience. Location may also be a factor within some industries. Consider the following niche markets that you can specialize in when starting your business.

Fresh Refrigerated Loads ("Reefer")

This is a great option for the new owner-operator. Within this section, the easiest industry to focus on is the meat and produce industries. There are many advantages to carrying these loads:

Fresh meat and produce are regularly transported, which means consistency.

Shippers are easy to find, from the local markets to wholesalers.

Loads in this area are resistant to recession, so you have revenue stability.

The bottom line is these loads also pay well, especially when you work directly with shippers.

Tankers

Both dry bulk and liquid tanker loads are profitable. Liquid tankers offer two separate options: food-grade liquids and hazardous materials. However, hauling these loads isn't easy and requires specific experience. There is also a higher cost of equipment when first getting started, especially for dry bulk equipment, which is very expensive.

Flatbeds

This is another area where you can focus since most large carriers avoid these loads. The difficult issue is finding a profitable load for both going out and backhauling. However, you can also find other opportunities.

Cattle and Livestock

Trucking businesses can also make a decent rate hauling livestock. Although these rates will largely depend on your location. If you live in an area that produces livestock, this can be a good option for an owner-operator who is just starting out and wants to stay local.

Once you have a plan in place, the most important step in starting your business is ready to begin. You'll now need to develop a business plan.

Create a Business Plan

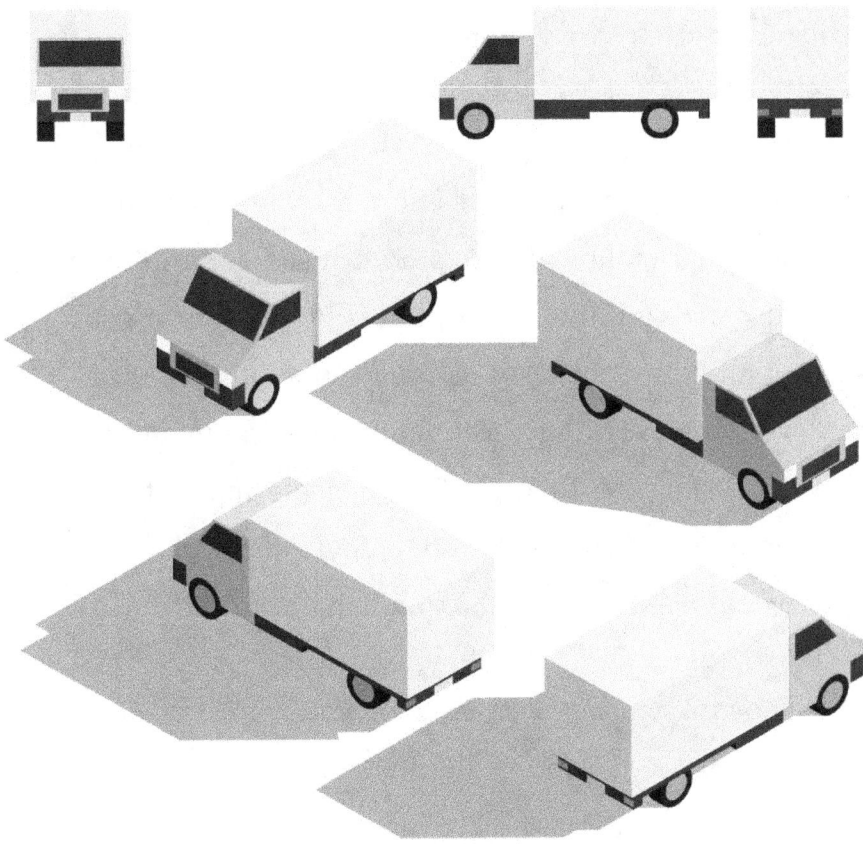

Before you start any business, it is important to have a business plan. It may not seem like you need to have a business plan for a trucking company since the underlying operating premises are straightforward. However, writing a business plan helps you focus on the core parts of your trucking company. It clearly shows you what your revenue and expenses are going to be. A good business plan provides the reason for starting your company, the capital needed to get started, financial projections with cost versus profits and other key strategy details.

When you have a business plan for your trucking business, you will be able to stay focused on building your company with a blueprint, which is helpful as you get started and may not have as much time to refocus on achieving your strategy. You'll also need a business plan in place if you plan to apply for any loan application to get funding for your business. When developing a business plan, you'll need to keep the following in mind:

• Knowing what trucking niche you want to focus on, such as a dry van, tanker, flatbed or other.

• Research any maintenance cost and durability of the common power units. Repair shops will charge different rates based on the engine and manufacturer. Finding the right balance will help reduce operating costs.

• Are certain permits and CDL endorsements required, such as hazardous materials.

- Do you need to purchase a trailer for the trucking niche you are focused on?

- Determine how much you need to set aside for operating costs and common maintenance needs like tires, oil changes and fuel.

- How big of a region will you operate in so you know how much you need to spend on specific permits.

A business plan should also project about three to five years ahead so you can get an idea of where your business is headed. Most business plans need to include the following:

- Executive Summary - Provides a short explanation about the company and your purpose for starting the business, as well as how you plan to achieve your business goals.

- Company Description - This description is specific to your company, including what it will do, what its mission is and what sets you apart from other short-haul trucking companies.

- Operations - This is everything related to the how of

your company, including technology, staffing and systems for operating the business.

• Services - What will your business offer to customers. It needs to be clear to both you and them.

• Market Analysis - Analyze what the current trucking market is like and how you plan to get your business to fit into it.

• Sales and Marketing - This is your strategy for bringing customers to your business.

• Financial Projections - Provide realistic expectations for revenue and profit as well as how you plan to meet these projections.

Here is a more in-depth look at the parts of a good business plan.

Executive Summary

In this section, you need to provide a short overview of your company and what you have planned for the future. The details in this section need to focus on the company mission, financial information, performance, and growth plans.

Ideally, this section should be no more than one to two pages. Since it is the first thing someone reads, you want to make a strong impression. The wording should be crisp, precise, and compelling. You want to grab the reader's attention and make a strong case for why your business will succeed. You want to make sure people will keep reading.

Company Description

In this section, you want to write about the background of your business and how you are connected to the industry. Add a little more detail about the company mission, how your business differs from others, and who your client base will be. Outline the advantages you have over competitors. You'll also want to include key facts about your business, such as the owners and management team, the year of incorporation, where you plan to operate, and the states you are registered in. If you have any employees, be sure to describe their roles and responsibilities here or discuss your plans to hire more drivers as your business grows.

Services

Here you'll want to outline what services you plan to offer, how you'll perform them, and how they will help to meet demand. Provide additional information on where you plan to operate and how it will influence your services. You'll also want to provide details on your pricing structure, the types of freight you'll haul, and which industries you'll serve.

Market Analysis

This is perhaps the most important section of your business plan. This is where you can attract lenders and investors based on your market knowledge. The goal is to provide the data that proves to potential investors that you know industry trends, market demand, and what works well and doesn't in the business to help you gain an advantage over competitors. A good market analysis section needs to include the following:

Industry Description and Outlook

Provide current data on the size of the trucking industry for carriers and dollars. Provide the number of competitors, the biggest carriers, the biggest shippers, and the annual revenue for the entire industry. You should also include data on how the industry is going to grow and evolve in five to ten years.

Target Market

Now you'll narrow the data to your specific niche market. Provide data in dollars, number of competitors, biggest shippers, and carriers. Include a market outlook for the next five to ten years. Also, show how you'll stand out from the competition when it comes to services, expertise, price, and reliability. Then provide data on how you'll plan to achieve success in a specified time period. The key is to be very specific.

Pricing and Margins

Detail how you'll price your services. Explain how it compares to your competitors and what kinds of margins are needed in order to operate at a profit.

Competitor Analysis

Potential investors want to know that you understand your competition in both carriers and owner-operators.

Provide details on the competition, including who their main customers are, what they do well, what their weaknesses are, and how you'll use these to your advantage.

Regulatory Environment

The federal government heavily regulates the trucking industry. There are limits on the number of hours you can drive, the types of material you can haul and where, fuel emissions, and the permits or licenses needed to operate. Explain what regulations you'll need to meet in order to run your business and how you plan to comply with them. You may also want to discuss operational risks and how they can impact your business.

Sales and Marketing

A key element to business success in any industry is to reach the right people at the right time. Convincing people to do business with you and establishing a relationship is key. In this section of your business plan, you need to discuss your strategies for finding potential customers and how you'll get them to use your services. You'll do this by including the following information:

Marketing Strategy

Here you'll explain what you plan to do to build and grow your client base. Provide a detailed plan for marketing your business and what tactics you'll use. Be specific about the potential clients you'll focus on and where you'll find them. Also, detail the budget you plan to set aside for your marketing efforts.

Sales Strategy

This section focuses on the types of sales operations you'll plan to set up. Provide details on who you'll hire for marketing or if you plan to do it yourself.

Funding Request

Here you'll detail your financing requirements or what you'll need to get your business running and operating into the future. You should be specific in terms of the money needed in the next several years and how it will be used. You need to also specify if you need debt or equity for how long and at what terms.

Financial Projections

This is where you'll get into the financial details of your company and how you plan to meet its fiscal targets. You'll want to include basic financial documents like a balance sheet, profit-loss statement, cash flow statement, and sales forecast. You should also have a break-even analysis to show what you need to sell both monthly and annually in order to cover the costs of doing business. End by providing an outlook of how your business is expected to perform in the next five years.

Once you have a business plan in place, you can start focusing on getting the necessary funds to start your business.

These are just the basics for writing a business plan. Always remember that the more research you do, the better your business plan will be. Once you have a business plan written, it is time to head to the third step in the process.

Register Your Business

Once you have a strong business plan in place, then you'll be ready to take the next step in starting your short-haul trucking business. This step requires you to register your business with any local and state governments that need it.

As you start your short-haul trucking company, you'll quickly find out that the most time-consuming part of the business is the paperwork needed to fulfill requirements set out by the FMCSA. While the process is time-consuming, it isn't that difficult. Depending on the type of short-haul trucking business you plan to start, you'll need to comply with most to all of the following:

- USDOT Number - This is used to collect and monitor safety information, inspections and crash investigations.

- Operating Authority - This determines the type of operation your company will run and the cargo it plans to carry.

- Heavy Vehicle Use Tax or Form 2290 - This is an annual federal tax for trucks over 55,000 pounds to help fund highway programs and improvements.

- Unified Carrier Registration or UCR - This system is designed to validate active insurance coverage within each state that you plan to operate your trucking business.

- International Registration Plan or IRP - This license allows your business to operate in all states of the United States, the District of Columbia and the provinces of Canada.

- International Fuel Tax Agreement or IFTA - This is a reciprocity agreement between the contiguous United

States and the Canadian provinces to simplify the reporting of fuel use by carriers who drive over multiple jurisdictions. Filings need to be done quarterly.

- BOC-3 Filing - This is a federal filing that assigns a process agent who will be served court papers during a legal proceeding. The process agent can be designated based on each state where you have an office or establish contracts.

- Drug Testing and FMCSA Clearinghouse - When all drivers are registered with the FMCSA Clearinghouse, it provides employers and government agencies with real-time data about drug and alcohol program violations by drivers. This information is helpful when completing insurance and licensing requirements.

When you start a short-haul trucking company, you should verify all licenses and permits needed for your business. Additional registrations may be required beyond this list, depending on the services you are going to provide and how you are going to operate your business. The FMCSA can help you streamline the process and navigate the filing requirements.

Business Structure

When registering your business, you also want to determine how your business will be structured. Two common structures for trucking businesses include the following:

1. Limited Liability Corporation (LLC)

2. Corporation (C-corp, S-corp, etc.)

Each of these business structures has their own advantages and disadvantages when it comes to liability and taxes. It can also vary based on the state where your business will be operating. If you aren't sure about the best business structure for your needs, then you may want to speak with an accountant.

When it comes to choosing a structure for registering and operating your trucking business, you have five options to choose from. Let's look at each of them to help you decide on what is best for you.

Sole Proprietorship

This is the least complicated option you can choose.

With this option, a single person owns and operates the entire company while also accepting all legal responsibilities. Rather than filing taxes as a business, the proprietor or owner will include them on their own tax return. The structure is relatively straightforward, so they are easy to set up and register. The main disadvantage of this structure is the liabilities. As a sole proprietor, you would personally accept any liability. This means that if a company or person were to take legal action against your company, then any cost of defense would come out of your own money.

Partnership

If you plan to start your business with other people, then you can register as a partnership. These can be both limited or general, each with their own pros and cons. A general partnership is almost the same as a sole proprietorship, except it is shared between two or more people. The business is an extension of the owners, and the owners take on all liability. Sharing liability with others can help lessen the blow of any legal action, making this option a little safer than a sole proprietorship. The other option is a limited partnership that involves a little more paperwork but provides the owners with a little more protection. In both options, the limited liability doesn't include personal assets.

LLC

An LLC or Limited Liability Company provides more legal protection than the previous two options. They often are formed separately from the owners so that if someone were to take legal action against your trucking company, the outcome would only affect the assets of the company and not your personal assets.

There are more steps involved in filing as an LLC, and you'll need additional documentation depending on your state. There is often a fee associated with submitting documents. Although there is more time and money involved upfront, the LLC provides a greater level of protection that can be helpful in the event of an accident. Trucking is a hazardous profession, and having this extra level of protection can be a good thing.

Corporation

As with an LLC, a corporation will require more documentation on the roles of people within the company. Corporations are made up of stockholders who own the company, directors who manage it, and officers who are responsible for the daily operations. If you want to file as a corporation, the company will often need to submit bylaws and articles of incorporation, but the final requirements will vary based on the state. There are also different types of taxes that apply to corporations than other types of businesses. However, these are one of the most complicated organizations to start when it comes to legal work, but in the end, you'll have the highest level of protection. If you plan to have multiple owners or expect substantial growth, then choosing to start a corporation might be the best choice for you.

ESOPs

When it comes to structuring a trucking company, another option is an ESOP or employee stock ownership plan. This option gives you fluidity and security. Through an ESOP, employees are given a stake in the company. Workers who are shareholders in a company are more likely to look out for the best interests of the company. Employees are also more likely to stay with your company longer and work towards its success. Trucking companies can sometimes have a higher burnout rate, but having a share in the company may encourage drivers to stay with you.

If, out of all these options, you choose to set up as a corporation or an LLC, then the next step you'll need to take is to appoint a registered agent.

In general, for self-owned trucking businesses, it can be a good idea to consider an LLC. This helps to protect your personal property and provide you with several tax advantages. When you form an LLC, most states will require you to appoint a registered agent. The registered agent is an individual who accepts and sends legal documents on behalf of your business. This individual will also receive compliance and tax information while being the direct point of contact for your business within the state.

In addition, for an LLC, you'll need to get an employer identification number or EIN. This number is required for any aspects of operation, including opening a business bank account.

Business Name

Along with registering your business and choosing a

business structure, you need to choose a unique business name. Your business name needs to be memorable since it is a crucial element of starting a successful trucking company. The business name is the first impression for potential clients, so it needs to communicate your brand, specialty and personality.

A unique name is needed for legal requirements, but a distinctive and easy to remember name is also important for marketing purposes. Keep in mind how you want your business perceived. Write down words that are commonly associated with your business on slips of paper and then mix and match them into different combinations to get some creative ideas. The name you choose should be relevant to trucking without being too lengthy, and it should also be translatable.

Lastly, business names can't be duplicated within the same industry or geographic location. Do a secretary of state and US Patent and Trademark search to make sure the name you want to choose is available for use.

Choosing to start your own trucking business is no easy decision or small task. Before you do anything else, you want to make sure you pick a name for your trucking company. This may seem like a simple and easy step, but it is actually a major decision and has a major impact on your business strategy. Consider the following tips to help you choose the best name for your trucking company.

Finding Ideas

Get together with family and close friends to brainstorm some ideas. Write down words that you think will describe your future business. Often involving others will help generate ideas you may not have thought about on your own. The important thing is to be as creative as possible and don't restrict yourself. You can narrow the list later; right now, you just want to write down everything that comes to mind.

Consider Your Goals

Consider what people will think of when they hear your business name. Is it the same as what you have in mind for your company? Does the name make your business south trustworthy and professional? Having a strong brand will depend on the strength of the name you choose, and it will have a big impact on marketing later on in the process. You can choose words that will attract the customers you want when you think about the goals you have for your trucking company.

Consider Your Business Structure

Depending on the business structure of your company, you'll likely need to have a corporate designation as a part of the name, such as Corp, Inc., or LLC. These naming requirements are used to help your customers know what type of business entity they are working with and reduce confusion.

It is also important that most states won't allow two trucking companies with the same name to operate, and some states won't even allow similar names. It is best to check the database for your state ahead of time to make sure you won't get a rejection for your business name. You should also be aware that some states will charge you to search the business name database. So have a couple of top choices in mind before you start your search.

Envision the Name

When you are thinking of names, be sure you also envision how it will look. This includes the side of your truck, any company logo, and on paperwork. You want something that isn't too long or complicated and can be easily stated over the phone. When choosing a name, you want one that will make it as easy as possible for you and your customers in the long run.

Unique Names

With hundreds of thousands of companies in the United States, it is safe to assume that most of the common trucking names are already taken. So take the time to consider how common your name is before committing to it. If you are committed to the name, then make sure you have a few unique alternatives to fall back on in case your first choice is already taken.

Logo Replicas

If you are going to develop a logo with your name, you want to avoid making a replica. The US Patent and Trademark Office offers a search tool so you can make sure your name and logo aren't too close to something that is already registered.

Family Names

Choosing a family name for your trucking company can

be a great way to build a legacy in the business. If you plan to start a family-run business and want to pass it on to the next generation, then you will want to choose a family name. Some customers might also enjoy working with a business more focused on family.

Location Names

If you plan to keep your trucking business within a specific geographical area, then you may want to consider a name based on the specific location. This name will also appeal to customers who want to hire local carriers. However, when choosing these names, also keep in mind any potential expansion plans since you don't want to limit yourself in the future.

Freight Type Names

If you are going to specialize in specific types of freight such as reefer, hazmat, or other types, then you may want to consider a name with this type of freight in it.

Unique Names

Lastly, if you want your company to stand out from the competition, then you may want to come up with a unique name. Perhaps one based on culture or personality. The focus will be on choosing a name that is memorable to customers.

Mistakes to Avoid

When it comes to choosing a name for your trucking business, there are three main mistakes to avoid. The first is to avoid choosing a name that is too common. The goal is to make customers remember you and common names will cause confusion. So avoid names that are too similar to other businesses.

Second, you want to avoid choosing a name that is a cliche. Don't choose words or expressions that aren't descriptive, and don't focus on the unique aspect of your business. Focus on positive words and metaphors that describe your company, and you'll find plenty of options to choose from.

Lastly, while you want to involve family and friends in choosing a name, you also don't want to involve too many people. This will give you too many options and can move you away from your business objectives. Rather just involve a few key people who know your goals and can help provide you with serious and strategic opinions.

From here, you are now ready to move on to the next stage of paperwork in the process of starting your short-haul trucking business.

Pushing Papers: Business Licenses, Permits, and Starting Costs

The next thing you need to do is make sure your business is ready to operate legally. To do this, you'll need to make sure you have the proper business licenses and permits.

Trucking businesses have unique challenges that face unique liabilities. This makes it important that you have all the required licenses and permits based on the state where your business will operate. Most states are going to require you to get a business license if you plan to headquarter your business within the state. All licenses and permits need to be set up before you take on your first shipment.

An important license you need to secure is an International Registration Plan. This license is required any time your truck is 26,000 pounds and crossing state lines. This license will allow you to operate your truck in all states and even Canadian provinces.

Since regulations will vary by state, you should consult your state's guidelines to determine exactly what you need to stay within local regulations.

Start-up Costs

Starting a short-haul trucking business will require a big up front investment to purchase a rig and trailer if needed. Plus, you need to cover the costs of licensing requirements and registration. In addition, experts recommend having enough money on hand for at least the first six months of operation, including any lease payments for your rig.

The price for a new commercial truck will start over $100,000 and can easily go to $200,000 based on make, model and features. Leasing costs can be $2,500 or more a month for a used truck and more than $3,500 a month for a new truck depending on interest and amortization. In addition to the truck, you need to factor the following into your business budget:

- Registration and documentation

- Permits and licenses

- Maintenance costs

- Accounting/invoicing software

As you can tell, the costs can easily add up. The average loan for a startup trucking business is about $100,000, according to the Small Business Administration. So knowing this, let's consider some financing options you have to help you get your business started.

Financing Options

There can be several options to help you get the funds

needed to start your short-haul trucking business. Consider the different options available to see which ones work for you.

Small Business Administration (SBA) Loans

SBA loans are a popular funding source for small businesses because of their low-interest rate and generous repayment terms. The only obstacle to getting these loans for your business is being able to qualify for them. You'll need an extensive credit history and a good credit score in order to get these loans.

Small Business Term Loans

With this funding arrangement, the lender provides a specific amount of money to you, and you repay it over time. Often these are faster than conventional loans. Qualification is easier than with an SBA loan, but the interest rates are higher and can be either fixed or varied. When it comes to funding options for a short-haul trucking business, this type of loan arrangement often isn't suitable for long-term planning.

Commercial Truck Financing

These loans are a great way to get the funds needed to buy new or used trucks. These are similar to a typical auto loan by using the vehicle as security for the loan. Payments are made monthly, and the financial health of the borrower will determine approval.

Freight Factoring

This is a highly popular funding source for trucking businesses at any point in their business development. It is an alternative form of financing that helps to accelerate cash flow and provide a constant access to working capital. Truck company owners gain a steady source of cash to support operational costs, pay bills, payroll and taxes by selling accounts receivable invoices at a discount. Each factored invoice becomes collateral for advancing funds to help eliminate the risk of losing higher-valued assets, which is the case when defaulting on a bank loan.

The main benefits of freight factoring is easy qualification for both new and established trucking businesses and to increase credit limits as the business grows. Capital will raise the industry standard for freight factoring services. Freight factoring provides money quicker with less hassle than traditional lenders.

Once you have the paperwork in order and have secured the necessary funds for starting your business, you can start planning your business operations.

Plan Business Operations

This next phase is the easiest since you've likely already been giving it a lot of thought. You need to plan out how your short-haul trucking business will operate. This includes all important issues, no matter how small. You'll need to ask yourself things such as the following:

• Where do you plan to park your truck and/or equipment when you aren't making deliveries?

• Who is going to be responsible for maintaining the equipment?

• How do you plan to find loads and orders?

• How are you going to handle back office duties such as invoicing, accounting, payroll and taxes?

Answering these and other questions related to the operations of your business can help you ensure you plan out the entire daily operations of your business so you won't be figuring things out at the moment.

Get Insurance

Insurance is likely going to be one of the biggest expenses for a new short-haul trucking business. When transporting freight, even for short distances, you'll need the following types of insurance:

• Primary Liability - In case of an accident, you want at least $750,000 in primary liability coverage to cover any damage or injury where you may be at fault. Some shippers or brokers will even require $1 million in primary liability coverage.

• Cargo - The most common request for covering cargo is $100,000, but this largely depends on the type of cargo you plan to haul. This insurance will cover both damage to the cargo as well as theft.

• Physical Damage - This insurance covers truck damage from accidents in which you aren't liable.

• Non-Trucking Use (Bobtail) - This insurance covers you if you are liable for an accident when you aren't hauling cargo for someone.

• Per-Load Insurance - You can use this to cut your annual insurance costs and cover specialty loads. It provides a cost effective and fast all risk smart coverage that you can get in less than 40 seconds.

You will need to get enough insurance to cover both your business, the equipment and the cargo you carry. At a minimum, the requirements for coverage are the following:

• Auto Liability

• Auto Physical Damage

• Cargo

• General Liability

If you are an owner-operator who is leased to another company's authority, then the average cost for insurance can be about $3,000 to $5,000 a year per truck. If you have your own MC authority, then the average cost for insurance is $9,000 to $12,000 a year per truck.

Buy or Lease a Truck

Aside from insurance, one of the largest investments you'll make when starting a short-haul trucking business is the commercial truck. This is going to be the backbone of your business, so it is key that you choose the right one for your needs. When choosing a commercial truck for your business, you'll want to consider the following:

- Price

- Comfort Level

- Preferred Cab Style

- Weather Resistance

- Dealership Locations

- Weight Limit

- New or Used

- Where you plan to operate

At this point, you should have already planned on the vehicle you need and just need to shop and make your equipment purchases. It is important to keep in mind that you likely aren't generating revenue at this point, so you don't want to overextend your start-up budget by purchasing things you don't need yet. This means the commercial truck you purchase needs to meet two main criteria:

1. Can it accommodate the cargo you plan to haul?

2. Is buying or leasing the best option for your business?

When it comes to purchasing a commercial truck and/or trailer, you should keep the following tips in mind:

• Used, older equipment may be cheaper to buy, but they are more expensive to maintain.

• Choose a commercial truck make and model that has a proven track record for fuel performance, durability and cheap maintenance costs.

• If you've worked as a company driver before starting your business, then consider the needs you've seen as well as consult the network of fellow drivers and mechanics you've developed before finalizing your commercial truck purchase.

• If you don't have the necessary cash reserves on hand to purchase a commercial truck, then consider the option to lease. Just keep in mind that the ongoing costs of leasing can affect your business. Be sure to research leasing practice, learn about the added costs and compare offers from a range of leasing companies before making a decision.

Keep in mind that once you have your business up and running, you can purchase additional items you need. So stick just to the basics as you're first getting started. Let's also take a closer look at the buying versus leasing option.

The buy versus lease debate for commercial trucks depends on your buying power as a new small business. There are several pros and cons to going each route. When buying a commercial truck outright, the payment is complete, and you won't have to keep making monthly payments. You can also have built-in equity to trade in the commercial truck in the future if you want to upgrade. However, keep in mind this will also mean a larger down payment of about 10 to 25 percent depending on whether you are purchasing a new or used commercial truck.

If you choose to lease, then you won't be owning the commercial truck. You'll need to make regular monthly payments, and you won't be able to use the equity to trade or purchase a new truck. You'll also need to follow specific regulations, such as maintaining the condition as well as mileage restrictions. However, there are some pros to leasing a commercial vehicle. The biggest of these is the fact that the lessor will often cover the cost of maintenance. If you choose to lease, be aware that there are several types of leases to consider:

• Operating (Full-Service) Lease - These leases require you to take care of maintenance, taxes and permits. Then at the end of the lease term, you simply walk away.

• Terminal Rental Adjustment Clause (TRAC) Lease - This lease requires a small down payment, and then at the end of the lease, you purchase the commercial truck for the residual value, or you can choose to have the leasing company sell the truck. If the leasing company makes money on the sale, then you get the profit, but if they lose money, then you need to pay the difference.

• Lease Purchase Plans - This option is primarily for truckers who either don't have the money for a down payment or have bad credit. With these arrangements, you'll often end up paying more compared to traditional financing.

Now you should be ready to start your business and get it up and running. Now the focus of your attention will shift to the day-to-day operations of your business. There are a few key areas that you need to focus on to ensure you stay within the rules of short-haul trucking. So let's take a look at how you can successfully operate and grow your short-haul trucking business.

Running a Short-haul Trucking Business

Once you've started a short-haul trucking company, the best advantage is that you can make business decisions based on the current economic conditions. High-cost trucking companies that have been in business awhile and expanded operations during the market frenzy of 2020-2021 may currently be worried about how they'll turn a profit. On the other hand, as a startup, you can set your business to run lean and maximize efficiency in order to give yourself a competitive advantage over these other businesses that may be bigger than your business.

The key to a successful short-haul trucking business is to maintain the proper balance between cost and revenue. You should base your business decisions on knowing what effect it has on costs. Charge customers enough to cover your expenses and still remain competitive, then drive as many loaded miles as possible. This may seem like a relatively easy balance to maintain, but it can be a little more challenging than it sounds.

As your business expands and grows, you'll need to focus more time and attention on keeping it running. This will increase the amount of activity you need to do. You'll need to look for loads, maintain pickup and delivery schedules, maintain compliance and many other distractions that will distract you from focusing on the financial responsibilities of your short-haul trucking business. The main problem to avoid is allowing the day to day operational issues to overwhelm you and to allow financial obligations to become a secondary situation. The key to running a successful short-haul trucking business is efficient accounts receivable management. You should bill customers as soon as deliveries are made, collect payments as soon as you can and make sure all your bills are paid on time.

In order to manage all these things while also building alliances and developing industry relationships with experts who can help your business succeed, you may need to end up working with a partner at some point. The best partner to hire is a financial partner who can manage your accounts receivables and make sure your business maintains a steady cash flow and turns a profit. To help you manage your short-haul trucking business and turn it into a success, you should consider the following tips:

- Keep good records of your income and expenses, such as insurance, legal fees and maintenance logs.

- Debt can make or break a small business so make sure you only borrow what you need when you need it.

- Make sure you review all shipments and consider the cost of maintaining your equipment, taxes, fees, fuel, tolls and other expenses in order to ensure you are taking on a profitable load.

- Ensure your business always has a healthy cash reserve to help cover unexpected repairs, employee time off and those times when you may have trouble finding a load.

• Consider using software programs that can help you optimize schedules, find profitable loads and increase the revenue stream for your business.

While these are all some good general tips for running the day-to-day operations of your short-haul trucking business, there are some very specific areas you need to focus on, and we'll discuss those next. This way, you can be sure your business continues to run as efficiently as possible and provides you the most profitable return on investment.

Stay Compliant

Transporting freight and the trucking industry is a highly regulated industry. As a short-haul trucking business owner, you need to comply with safety and government regulations if you want to stay in operation. This means you need to stay current with time sensitive filing requirements that range from the IFTA's quarterly tax returns to multi-year renewals for CDLs. If you don't keep up with the necessary requirements, then you'll not only lose your good standing with these organizations, but you'll also face heavy penalties. The FMCSA has a registered filer program on their website that can help you stay up to date. If you want to help your business have long-term success, then you need to maintain compliance with both state and federal regulations. Some tips for this include the following:

• Make sure you keep track of all expiration and renewals dates for any regulatory processes such as licenses, permits, filings and insurance.

• If paperwork needs to be kept within the commercial truck, then make sure it is in an accessible and easy to remember location so anyone driving the truck knows where to find it should someone ask.

• Make sure you follow safe vehicle operations at all times. This includes following hours of service regulations, weight restrictions and other safety requirements. If you don't follow these regulations, then it will have a negative impact on your CSA safety score and prohibit you from hauling loads for certain shippers that require high safety scores.

The last thing you can afford to have happen as a small

business owner is to head for a scheduled pick-up only to find out you are being placed out of service for non-compliance and faced with a heavy fine to pay. This can have a bad impact on your relationship with customers, add more expenses to your new small business and potentially even shutter your business permanently. Therefore, it can be a good idea to simply review your documents on a regular basis to ensure you are staying compliant and avoiding detrimental issues for your short-haul trucking business.

Along with staying compliant, it is a good idea to make sure you have an understanding of the short-haul exemptions that can make compliance a little easier for your business.

Short-haul Exemptions

In 2017, the Federal Motor Carrier Safety Administration or FMCSA enacted the Electronic Logging Device or ELD mandate. This mandate required carriers and drivers to use ELDs to record their hours of service or HOS. Then in 2020, the HOS was amended to improve safety for everyone on the road by ensuring drivers accurately track, manage and share their duty status records. While these rules apply to many in the trucking industry, they don't apply to all trucking businesses. If you are going to run your own short-haul trucking business, then you need to know who qualifies for short-haul exemption based on the rules and how this can affect your business. So let's take a moment to help you understand these rules and exemptions.

What is the Exemption to the Rules?

The short-haul exemption is a limited exemption to the rule that requires drivers to track their activity with an electronic logging device. Short-haul ELD exemptions are available to some carriers as long as the short-haul trucking business meets the necessary criteria. This is because the FMCSA, under the direction of the US Department of Transportation or DOT, determined that there is less concern about short-haul drivers working extended hours and traveling longer distances than long-haul drivers. This eliminated the requirement for ELD logging for specific hours of service regulations. This exemption can be referenced under several names, including the following:

• The FMCSA short-haul exemption

- DOT short-haul exemption

- ELD short-haul exemption

No matter what you call this short-haul exemption, it is important to know whether your business and drivers qualify under the DOT short-haul rules. If you don't quality for the exemption and fail to follow proper ELD rules, then your business can face fines, drivers can be placed out of service, your CSA scores can be affected, and both drivers and carriers can be subject to prosecution.

How the Exemption Works

If your drivers or business meets the requirements for the short-haul exemption, then you won't need to use an ELD as required under the FMCSR code. In addition, drivers who qualify for the short-haul exemption don't need to comply with the code that mandates a 30 minute break in driving status after eight hours of driving.

Who Qualifies for the Short-haul Exemption?

In order to qualify for the short-haul exemption, drivers need to meet a specific series of requirements. Let's look at each of these to help you understand if your drivers meet these exemptions.

Mileage Limits

Short-haul drivers aren't allowed to travel routes that extend beyond a specific mileage limit from their starting position. The DOT classifies these as "air miles", which is defined as a straight line between two specific points on a map, whether it happens to be a direct route or not. For an driver operation as an interstate carrier with a commercial driver's license, the limit is 100 air miles. For a non-CDL driver, the limit is 150 miles, and the drivers aren't allowed to pass through any state that requires a CDL for their vehicle.

Hours of Service

The second requirement is that drivers can't exceed 11 straight hours of driving and need to officially clock out and be off duty within 12 hours of starting a shift. This means that the individual can't work in any other capacity as a driver; this includes maintenance or inspections. Drivers are also required to have at least 10 straight hours of off-duty time between shifts.

Starting and Ending Points

Another requirement DOT short-haul rules require drivers to start and end their hauls at the same location. No matter what the distance traveled, if short-haul drivers start at your business facility and end at another, then they aren't exempt unless they are able to return to their starting location at the end of the day. This specifically excludes long-haul drivers.

Recording and Record Retention

Lastly, if you qualify for the short-haul exemption under the FMCSA rules to the ELD mandate, then you are also not required to use an electronic logging device. However, your short-haul trucking business will still be required to keep records of working hours. These records would include the following:

- The time a driver reports for duty each day.

- The total number of hours a driver is on duty each day.

- The time drivers go off duty each day.

• The total driving time for drivers within the previous seven days.

As a part of your fleet management, you should retain driver records proving that all operators were following HOS regulations. These records should be kept for a period of at least six months. Driver records that are required by the FMCSA exemption are separate from Record of Duty Status or RODS and need to be maintained by the carrier or company. Drivers don't need to keep RODS specifically based on the DOT short-haul exemption rules.

Qualifying for Short-haul Exemptions

As long as drivers meet the above requirements, then they can qualify for short-haul exemptions. Under specific circumstances, there are some other exceptions to the ELD mandate, including the following:

• Drivers with a vehicle that has a model year or engine from 1999 or earlier. This is because most of these vehicles don't have ELD port connections.

• Any driver who is required to keep their logs for more than eight days in a 30 day period. A short-haul driver may travel beyond the 100 or 150 air-mile radius, but if it is infrequent then they can be exempt. Infrequent is defined as no more than eight times in a 30 day period.

• Under some circumstances, driveaway and/or tow-aways operations are exempt. If the commercial vehicle being driven is being delivered or if the driver is transporting an RV trailer or motorhome with wheels, then they may be exempt

What If You Don't Qualify for the Exemption?

If your drivers or business doesn't currently qualify for the short-haul exemption under the rules, then you have a few options to consider. The first option is to purchase and install electronic logging devices in order to maintain compliance with the ELD mandates and HOS rules. While there will be an initial cost for purchasing and installing these devices, it would be the easiest way to ensure your business is complying with the rules and ensures you are following all regulations under DOT and FMCSA rules.

Another option is to update any short-haul routes to make sure they fall within the target radius, and drivers follow any other requirements to comply with the short-haul exemptions. Keep in mind that even if your drivers or business qualifies for the ELD exemption, motor carriers and owner-operators are still required to comply with HOS requirements and to record and maintain the necessary paperwork.

It is important that you plan ahead. Take a few moments to plan how conditions can have an impact on short-haul exemption rules. This can have a big difference. For example, you can do some of the following:

• Check your maps and GPS for road closures, traffic hotspots or backups that can increase the number of driver hours on the road.

• Call ahead to your destination to ensure they won't have any extended wait times when the drivers arrive.

• Know the best places to fuel up in order to limit unnecessary miles and save your business money.

• Adjust drivers' individual workloads in order to meet shift requirements.

It is also very important that you stay up to date with

the FMCSA short-haul exemption rules. FMCSA rules are prone to change at any time, and the best way to ensure you stay in compliance is to keep up to date on any change to the regulations. Drivers should also stay informed at all times of the current rules so they can follow regulations. You should also consider having your drivers get regular training to ensure they are completely aware of the driving requirements.

Should You Get an ELD Even if You're Exempt?

Even if your fleet meets the requirements for an ELD exemption, you may want to consider using an ELD anyways. There are three categories of fleets that should consider using an ELD even if they are exempt under the rules.

If You Are Planning to Grow Your Business

If you are currently planning to grow your business or expect it to grow within the next year, then you may want to start using an ELD or other solution. Doing the initial implementation is often easier when you have a smaller fleet of vehicles and drivers then you can scale up as your business grows.

If You Want to Reduce CSA Violations

Even if you are exempt from ELD requirements, using a telematics solution throughout your fleet will help your total CSA score by keeping you more aware and alert of the activities within your fleet, such as frequent speeding and hard braking.

If Your Business Has Multiple Drivers

If your short-haul trucking business has multiple drivers or vehicles, then you will get a faster return on your financial investment if you implement a telematics solution despite being exempt from ELD requirements.

This brings us to the operations portion of your business, that focuses on establishing a fleet management process.

Establish a Fleet Management Process

When you start a short-haul trucking business, you

also need to know how to manage vehicle maintenance, stay in compliance with regulatory and safety requirements, manage fuel and supervise drivers. Managing these areas can become even more challenging as your business grows and you add more trucks to build your fleet. You can take away some of this by using fleet management software. No matter what, you'll need to find a way that allows you to manage the day to day operations of your business operations. A part of this is knowing how to find and get the most profitable loads.

Getting Loads

After you've started your business, the key part of keeping it running is to get profitable loads. Without loads, your business won't be able to make money. As a short-haul business, you have three main options for finding a profitable load:

1. Load Boards - Think of these as a classified ad for the trucking industry. Shippers and brokers post loads on these boards, and then owner-operators can choose when loads they want to take.

2. Shipper Relationships - This method can sometimes

cause delays in getting your first load if you haven't previously developed a network of shippers. However, if you developed your network while initially gaining your driving experience with a company, then you may already have a network of shippers to get loads from.

3. Freight Brokers - This is the surest way to find a load, but you'll have to give about 25 to 50 percent of your revenue to the broker. So you would be undercutting the potential profits for your startup business.

No matter which of these methods you use, you will need a strong cash reserve since it can take up to 45 days to get paid for your first load and any subsequent load. This is why you need an understanding of how freight payments are processed and what potential delays can occur. You should also anticipate and cover your expenses while waiting for these accounts to settle so your business can remain in operation.

After you've developed a good working day to day operation for your business, then it is time to consider the option of growing and building your business. Let's look at some ways you can do this.

Build Your Business

A critical aspect of your new business success is building long-term sustainability. To do this, you need to diversify and expand your customer base to ensure continued long-term success of your short-haul trucking business. The best rule of thumb to follow is that a single customer shouldn't represent more than 20% of your revenue to avoid putting all your eggs in one basket. You should always be looking for new sources of freight. In order to do this, you can consider some of the following tactics:

- Load Boards

- Freight Brokers

- Business Networking

- Referrals

- Collaborative Partnerships

- Media Advertising

- Social Networking

However, this doesn't mean you can neglect or simply drop a customer after a single load. You also need to focus on retaining customers and growing your business through superior customer service. To do this, you need to plan, execute and optimize the shipment of cargo, keep customers informed of exactly where their shipments are and monitor on-time performance in order to meet or exceed customer expectations. This is the most effective way to grow and maintain a profitable short-haul trucking business.

Conclusion

Whether you're just starting out getting your experience working for a carrier, starting your new business as the sole driver or expanding a successful short-haul trucking business and spending less time on the road, the key to being successful in the trucking industry is to maintain a good work-life balance. Let's finish by providing some ways that you can successfully manage a work-life balance.

Anyone who works as a truck driver will face a unique set of challenges when it comes to maintaining a work-life balance. In order to better define your goals and work towards a healthy work-life balance as a short-haul truck driver, you should first consider the challenges you'll face:

- Being away from family

- Being away from friends

- Safety and compliance on the road

- Unhealthy food options while driving

- Unusual sleep patterns

- Unusual work schedules

- City ordinances that limit commercial vehicle travel

- Legal status, such as married versus single

While there isn't a single specific solution to maintain a healthy work-life balance while driving commercial trucks, there are plenty of options that can help. The following are some ideas that can help you manage your work-life balance, but nothing is going to be specific to every person or job duty, so you can be creative in finding the ideal solution that works for your individual situation.

Consider a Flexible Schedule

Creating a more flexible schedule can help you to be home for special occasions. Whether you work for a company or are an owner-operator, you should communicate with your broker or dispatcher when you'll be unavailable. These individuals can help you and will often work with you to develop a flexible schedule that promotes a healthier work-life balance. If a company or business isn't willing to work with you and your scheduling needs, then you may want to consider making a necessary change.

Plan Your Routes

When you plan your route in advance and stick to it, you will be able to have a positive impact on your work-life balance. Keep in mind that you aren't bound to your commercial truck. Plan your route in such a way that you may be able to try new restaurants or visit a place of interest as you make your deliveries throughout the day. If you work as a ride-sharing service or taxi service, you can even consider a night out on the town, visiting historic landmarks or doing anything else that can help promote a healthier work-life balance.

Learn Something New

Whether it be courses on audiobooks, college lectures, podcasts or anything else, driving a trucking route gives you the unique opportunity to expand your horizons and learn something new while still performing your daily job duties. There are plenty of content providers for educational content that provide an endless choice of subjects to learn on.

Home Cooked Meals

Consider packing a home cooked meal to eat while you're on the road rather than always eating out. Not only can this save you money, but it can also be a healthier option that reminds you of home. If the situation allows, you can even bring the ingredients, utensils and equipment in the truck with you and prepare a fresh meal from the comfort of your truck while making your daily deliveries.

Use Tools

Consider finding and using tools that will automate some of your business processes that would otherwise take you and your drivers longer to do. For example, there are software programs that can help you create the optimal schedule in only three minutes. This is a fraction of the time it would take you to do it yourself.

Pick up a Hobby

Consider taking up a hobby you can practice while on the road so you can take your mind off work once you're done for the day. Some popular options are things like photography and journaling. As a truck driver, you'll experience a lot of sources of inspiration from landscapes to people. Working with a hobby provides you with a way to relax, keep your mind sharp and focused while also allowing you an interesting way to document the places you've been. Whatever allows you to wind down and blow off steam after a long day driving on the road can help you reduce stress and improve your work-life balance.

Make Sure Your Company Supports You

Nothing can have a bigger impact on your work-life balance than the company you drive for. You want to choose a business that supports you and cares about your wellbeing. This can make all the difference in your work-life balance. With the demand for truck drivers on the rise, you can easily choose who you want to work for. Look for a business that lets you choose your own loads and create your own schedules based on needs and preferences.

Stay Connected with Family and Friends

Even if you are home by the end of the day, it is still a good idea to stay connected to family and friends by calling and checking in throughout the day. Smartphones, laptops and wireless internet access makes this possible whether you are at a rest area or truck stop. So make a video call, send a text message or email, share pictures and anything else that helps you feel more connected to home.

Make Sure You Take Care of Yourself

Truck driving can actually be very hard on the body, and it can be difficult to maintain a healthy lifestyle while on the road. So make sure you have a good diet and exercise routine with adequate rest. It is also important that you attend to your personal hygiene so you'll have both a healthy and happy work-life balance. You can also help your mood by finding ways to meditate and relax.

Share Your Schedule

Make sure you keep your family and friends in the loop since this is important for you and your families work-life balance. While your family is home and you're on the road, you should make sure your family is aware of your schedule.

Create a calendar you can share with your family and provide them with location updates so you know when you'll be gone and when to expect you home. This can also be a good safety measure so someone always knows where you are should something happen.

Have a Good Sleep Space

If you happen to spend multiple days on the road, then a sleeping berth will become your home away from home. Make sure you keep it as clean and comfortable as possible. Have a comfortable mattress, clean sheets, personal photos and other home reminders so you get plenty of good rest. This will also help keep you safe while driving since you'll be well rested.

Take Breaks and Have a Vacation

Make sure you take a break whenever you feel you need to. While driving, it is a good idea to take regular breaks to stretch and avoid injury. If you're hungry, take the time to get some food. If you feel tired, make sure you catch up on sleep. Also, make sure you know when it's time to take a vacation and give yourself adequate time off to decompress and spend time with your family or just to get away from it all for a bit.

Truck driving can be a challenging profession and an even more challenging industry. It will ask a lot of you as a driver and a business owner. However, it is also a rewarding and fun job.

It allows you to have control not only over your daily work life but also your personal life as well. So with some planning, practice and work, you'll be able to have a good work-life balance and a successful short-haul trucking company.

So if this still seems like a good career choice for you, then use the steps in this book to help you get on the way to starting a short-haul trucking business. You'll be glad you did as you start enjoying the freedom of driving the open roads and running your own business, which gives you better control over your work-life balance.